The Art Of **HYBRID** War

J.J. Patrick

First published in the United Kingdom 30th April 2018 by

The Art Of Hybrid War

The Art Of Hybrid War is a work of non-fiction, reflecting on the philosophy of modern asymmetric warfare, meditating on the meaning of real events, and taking some inspiration from the ancient Chinese texts attributed to Sun-Tzu in the Art Of War - freshly interpreted through new and freely available technology.

Cynefin Road is a small, independent publishing house and a champion of Copyright, so thank you for buying an authorised edition of this book and refusing to feed the pirates (not the rum loving kind) by copying, scanning, or otherwise distributing this brilliant tale without permission. It also means you'll steer clear of the long arm of the law and without you being a goody two-shoes, we wouldn't be able to bring you amazing things to read. Writers deserve your support and ours, so give yourself a pat on the back for doing something wonderful and enjoy the story.

Knowing you've read this small print makes us happy enough to throw some shapes while nobody's watching. We hope you have a nice day, wish you multiple lottery wins, and want you to find infinite joy wherever life's rich journey may take you.

First Edition

ISBN 978-1-9997854-6-8

This work would not have been possible without the kind support of its patrons:

Chris Durham, Carol Croft, Eugenio Mastroviti, Sonia Alani, Peter Rouch, Andrea Fairhurst, Geoffrey Brown, Nick Hennessey, Julia Stevenson, Laura Timoney, Jamie Duxbury, James Tindall, Stephen Cosgrove, Lindleywood, Simon Ferris, Martin Colston, Michael Torr, Helen Rees, Gerard Redmond, Emma Knuckey, Gary Weston, Angel Kiddy, Chris McCray, Alan Selby, Dai Jenkins, Christine Tennant, Chris Pitts, Bill Brown, Andrew Rigg, Angela Marston, Anna Spiteri, Paul Ellis, Roy Hall, Jane Gould, Charles Thompson, and Catherine Pickersgill.

PREFACE

Not all soldiers are warriors and not all warriors are soldiers.

People face battles every single day, and not all of those fights involve bullets and bombs. Though that is not to say the peril is any the lesser. Some face their own demons. Some face the situational asphyxia of life. Poverty, domestic violence. Abuse. Others face the consequences of arms sales and oil wars. Territorial conflicts founded upon little more than greed and ego. Motivations as old as recorded history itself. But this book concerns war. The very art of it once meditated upon and set down by Master Sun-Tzu hundreds of years before we defined an epoch with the birth of a mythical being and reset the clocks. Time's hands have since ticked by and we now face a very different world — one where swords have been replaced by weapons of mass destruction and computers, and battlefields have shifted from the blood-soaked mud to the dirty code of the online world.

Having been familiar with the Lionel Giles translation of The Art Of War for some years, and having read the more recent interpretations of Ralph D. Sawyer and John Minford, I returned to numerous, freely available online versions of the original Chinese writings (now over two thousand years old) and spent hours using translation software of varying brands to meditate on the raw text — setting it against the contemporary backdrop of malware, critical infrastructure hacks, new military theory, and complex disinformation warfare to create this fresh work.

We appear to have a great deal more to reflect upon at this juncture yet, in truth, so little has changed. Barring, of course, an accelerated shrinkage of the world through the erosion of defined borders — a blurring of nations and territories into little more than bytes and connection speeds. Humans are as pliable as ever, war just as contemptuous of us. While soldiers and warriors may not be the same thing, war has done little more than change its clothes.

The Art Of Hybrid War is, in some ways, an adaptation of Sun-Tzu's ancient teachings, set against a world he would not have recognised — one even we only thought we understood. In the main, however, this my own meditation on the doctrines of war which envelope all modern theatres of conflict, from the Soviet era and the much later Capstone Concept, written by NATO, to the electoral interference and voter suppression seen across the West – from Brexit to Trump, and beyond.

I hope you find some equilibrium resides among these words.

J.J. Patrick – January to April 2018

POLARISE OPINION.

GLAMORISE EXTREMES.

SALT THE COMMON EARTH.

Bros

1.1 War is a truth unchanged in millennia.

A steel and fire beast.

Mother of both life and death.

An engine of destruction,

in which the pistons are fired to a white-hot glow.

Fuelled by competing forces of extinction and survival,

the vacuum a conflict of humanity.

Of desperation and desire.

Only its devices evolve.

War and peace exist by the eternal fear at the dark
heart of every nation,

the former a tinderbox which must be delicately carried
by all leaders.

For, otherwise, Earth is destined to wildfire.

Cities to ruins.

Life to ash.

1.2 No light contemplation,

decisions of war must stand on all of the central
columns.

The opened tinderbox must balance upon each,

atop the weight of closely measured circumstance.

Centred in the combative compass of winds.

These immovable stone pillars are known by many names,

yet their cores remain constant.

Timeless.

The message,

the spiritual,

the reality,

the discipline,

and the authority.

These are the pillars of war.

1.3 The message provokes the meeting of the people and the state,

on a road all will travel without faltering,

to death or to victory.

A crafted and curated will of the people,

whatever its true meaning may be.

1.4 The spiritual presents a manufacture of balance

between harm and good.

The creation and recreation of what is right and what is wrong.

Fabrication of values and virtues through the existence of some higher power,

to which authority is always nearest.

To which authority alone holds the key to understanding,

whether its divinity derives from religion or government or corporation,

and to the word of which the people voluntarily bow in deference.

1.5 The reality is the assessment of the terrains and landscapes of war.

Networks and nodes.

Logistics and transportation and infiltration and extraction.

Sub-ocean cables and enabled devices and clouds.

Oil and gas and minerals and code.

Cartography of a world without borders defined by chains of supply and demand.

The reality is an understanding of not only Earth's

cycles,

but the viral ebbs and flows of human behaviour.

Income and expenditure and profit and loss.

Wants and desires.

These are the conditions under which war will be
fought and hearts won,

or resistance defeated.

The ecology of humanity.

Reality is to grasp more than victory herself.

It is to understand acceptable loss through the measure
and calculation of risk.

1.6 The discipline of war is not the base control of
instinct and behaviour alone.

Nor solely the rigid upkeep of financial accounts,

balancing books on the jagged surfaces of war.

Rather,

it is maintenance of structure and a defined chain of
command,

from the front lines to the hidden facilities,

which endures endless decapitations.

An immortal Hydra.

1.7 The authority is born from the ability to command the knowledge of reality.

To invoke the message without hesitation or fear of consequence.

To harness the spiritual in creation of values,

and to maintain mastery of its divine mystery.

To maintain the discipline,

never displaying any perceptible loss of control,

even slight or momentary.

To stay within the structures of law domestically and internationally,

by any margin, slim or wide,

or not at all,

by remaining an unseen shadow,

unbound by legal shackles.

1.8 Every leader, at every level, must balance the tinderbox on these columns.

Must know these pillars as well as their own hands.

One who does so is victorious in war.

Those who fail to understand and maintain these principles are defeated,

doomed to bitter loss before the grim dance even begins.

1.9 In the preparations for war,

in assessing the circumstance and conditions under which the tinderbox opens,

consideration must be given to who has:

Met the people with the message,

and defined a consensus,

and possesses authority capable of harnessing the fabricated will.

1.10 Consideration must be given to:

Which party has balanced the spiritual scale and seen to the reality of war.

Whether the discipline is sufficient,

controlled with iron grip,

or is weaker than that of the adversary.

Who holds the largest stockpiles of weaponry,

and the means to manufacture during conflict.

Who understands that modern weaponry is constrained only by imagination.

Which side has the resources and resilience to fall upon in hardship.

1.11 In the preparations for war,

consideration must also be given to which party to the confrontation has:

Established the most efficient system of punishment for failure,

and reward for compliance.

Which side fears most for reasons of internal consequence.

1.12 From this assessment of the whole,

victory or defeat can be predicted in anticipation of any confrontation.

Those who exist in perpetual readiness are victorious,

being at war even when peace deafens.

The ill-prepared are destined to defeat,

hearing nothing until marching boots arrive as thunder.

The unprepared cede to irrecoverable destruction with every breath taken.

This is war.

Its consequence deniable only to the fool.

1.13 The state which balances best upon the columns lays plans,

to reserve and deploy that which it already possesses,

while concentrating on the identification of what it does not yet have.

Anticipates advantages to be gained.

Prepares in advance the opportunities to attain them.

Foresees the losses it could inflict,

and acts ruthlessly to bring them about.

The tide of war is this:

Capitalise and Exploit.

Exploit and Capitalise.

1.14 The fires of war burn brightest on coals of deception.

The pretence of incapability when it is not a transparent deceit.

The disguise of deployments through alternative appearance.

Detached and deniable assets.

Appearing distant when you are the breath on the enemy's neck.

Ensuring your threat appears imminent when it is not.

Claim victimhood.

Play dead.

Loose apparitions of your defeat to secure glory.

1.15 Conquest is assured for the party who considers war with this utmost care,

even before a single arm is raised.

Defeat is guaranteed to the careless,

who fail to balance the tinderbox,

and dismiss an adversary without due comprehension of the threat posed.

If the enemy is resilient be alert.

If it shows great strength do not engage.

When they are weakened,

incite false pride.

Nationalism.

When they are calm,

create fluster.

Populism.

Assault every weakness in their defences,

military or civil.

Strike everywhere they have not anticipated attack.

Seek every seam,

every pressure point.

Democracy is riddled by its very nature.

If the people are united,

create fractures.

Drive silken wedges deep into the slimmest fissure.

Drip with honey.

Divide with whispers.

Disrupt with madness.

Conquer with velvet.

This is glory in war.

A victory unseen until it is complete.

PARAMETERS

2.1 A force of any measure will fall,

unless it has been provisioned to endure a campaign transcending tradition.

Designed for conflict deeper than man's darkest dream,

fought on grounds which do not yet exist.

Yet victory must be lightning.

A cobra's bite.

For morale erodes with time.

The will of the people falters.

Morale plummets in short order,

without a declaration of battle won.

A stalemate saps nerve.

Discipline is strained by the advance of time,

and even hidden war chests deplete readily without rapid conquest.

2.2 It is long said of war to make haste is the fool's act.

But action unduly withheld,

a stutter,

to say the least,

is unwise.

No country has ever reaped harvest from prolonged struggle.

Nor from hesitation.

A nation tires and collapses in a blink alone.

Exhausted forces,

a weakened will,

and stretched finances,

open the gates to feral rebellion.

Through this lowered drawbridge an intuitive enemy will set to you,

returning the venom of your intent,

and even the great empires will face nothing but defeat,

powerless to rally.

So cast away from drawn conflicts.

Pursue swift triumphs.

Move.

Shift.

Set pace rather than keep time.

Define agility.

2.3 Fill war chests with finances for home's pleasures,

and expenditures beyond domestic borders alike.

War is a balanced force

of internal and external counterweights.

Its base need constant at origin and destination.

Defend economy at all costs,

having built it beyond war alone.

Surrender neither ground,

nor ally,

for folly or nostalgia.

Only the weak sell the tools and weapons of war in faraway lands,

while creating a cheapened and doomed fleet to protect home waters.

2.4 Loss awaits nations of warmongers not warriors.

Fantasist historians arming potential enemies.

Sunset empires,

little more than assets to strip when real war comes.

For these peoples,

war itself can no longer be deemed as understood.

These are dead stars.

2.5 Embrace partnerships in the underworld,

unholy alliances built upon pacts of blood.

Harness extremism,

its secret power bases.

Money and influence.

Fill the swamps.

Influence money.

Grease the palms that grease the wheels.

Extend your reach to both the heights and the depths,

and expand beyond control of law.

Hide finances in the shadows of cryptography,

darken your economy to watching eyes.

Launder and be mindful,

measuring the world exchanges at all times,

to preserve strength of currency -

the ability to buy information, contacts, and access;

to innovate and make repairs;

to upgrade the tools of war.

Never embrace isolation,

nor risk all on dreams of days of yore.

Play the future.

Game the systems.

Influence market peaks and troughs through assets and events.

In readying for one war hold the secret coffers full for ten.

For any campaign must turn its profit,

through acquisition of benefit and causation of loss.

Place all bets not by odds but brutal design.

Pilot rather than navigate.

The wise leader holds the future as a private treasure and a public boast.

Fates of nations,

jeopardy and serenity,

theirs to control.

2.6 In times of war,

forbid continued transportation of supplies to the fronts.

Ensure troops are deployed equipped beforehand,

but only sufficiently to force continued scavenge.

To leech from the enemy.

Breed ingenuity.

Forces are fuelled this way,

for supply,

when continuous,

is a mark of no discipline.

This weakness is gluttony,

and such fat deployments generate inflation.

Rising prices empty pockets,

and at home families suffer

On the fields woeful soldiers are sapped of emotional strength.

The internal and external wars are lost in unison,

as drained finances weaken the message.

As deficits breed poverty.

In turn eroding faith.

And though home's spending is arrested,

war's hunger continues devouring taxes and levies.

The public purse spirals.

Grinding halt awaits any such march.

The wise leader knows this hateful lover,

and nurses on his enemy's teat.

2.7 One ration held by an adversary is worth twenty times a home provision.

One bullet from a rival cache is a magazine carried to the front.

The forage,

the hunt,

the key to war's bounty.

And a prize must be offered for capture

of tools and weapons from the enemy.

Praise heaped upon the soldier who is champion in scavenge.

For murder is born of rage.

Passion.

But war must be cold,

as soldiers loins are unheated in battle.

The desire for plunder is more easily birthed,

where immediate reward becomes the prize.

So starve your forces to winter their souls,

for necessity breeds dispassion.

Conflict conducted as ice.

The foe must be shown these spoils on display.

Must see their own arms used against them,

recognition destroying spirit.

Your army must feast while their cupboards are bare
and stomachs empty.

Flags must fall before their eyes.

Minds must be broken.

Yet captives must be met with heart.

Disarmed with care.

Bring them to you.

Raise them up.

Swell your ranks.

2.8 In war numbers are everything,

yet count for nothing.

Ten thousand soldiers no match for the mother of
bombs,

a thousand bombs no match for the few lines of code
which launch them.

OPERATING SYSTEM

3.1 The smouldering ruin,

the smoking crater,

the charred and blackened,

infertile husk,

are no prize worthy of the warrior.

Superiority in war is attained by the taking of a nation intact.

Rich.

Functional.

Plucked from the harrying winds all but unscathed.

Resources to be harvested,

only chaos to sooth.

And this ancient wisdom never changes suit.

Ever was it superior

to capture a unit,

a company,

a division,

brigade or battalion,

or army,

whole rather than decimated.

3.2 The mathematics of war remain stone tablets:

with ten times the force,

surround your foe where they sleep.

Five times the force,

assault your enemy where he stands.

Twice the force,

pincer your adversary.

Divide and conquer.

A matched force

sees nothing but the brutal confrontation of tooth and nail.

Where your enemy has greater numbers,

bide your time.

Hidden.

When you are weaker still,

flee.

For even the skilled and stubborn will be defeated,

when they are few standing against many.

Thermopylae an ancient testament,

misunderstood by countless passers-by.

Mastery of war is not emerging from the battle bloodied,

but overwhelming an adversary without physically engaging.

3.3 Warfare cascades as a waterfall.

The crest:

the offensive against strategy itself.

The assault on affinity and union.

Polarise opinion.

Glamorise extremes.

Salt the common earth.

Destroy centres of balance.

Below:

the attack on military forces.

The angry white-water fall in which all is lost.

A headlong charge against the people and their cities.

The base:

siege,

below the roiling water.

A suffocating victory of preparation and slow advance.

Only authority afflicted with unconquered rage,

the red mist of quick temper,

rashly deploys their force against fortifications.

Futile waves destined to break and ebb.

A war fought this way is drowning by thirds.

Breathe free and fight at the crest.

Always.

3.4 Those who master the cascade conquer the fields without blood spilled,

take the ground avoiding suffocation,

and defeat their enemies before the hourglass turns.

3.5 Those who strive for excellence in war

emerge from battle unmarked.

Objectives met.

Prizes claimed.

Blades sharp and powder dry.

Without a bullet fired.

3.6 Leadership in war is the fulcrum.

When strong,

the people can pivot.

May be freely levered to the needs of conflict.

Weak leadership collapses the mechanism:

tampering in the decisions of war without
understanding its art,

misdirecting forces and distracting strategists,

installing the inexperienced or inappropriate in power
positions.

Bewildering earned prowess with the ill-conceived ideas
of novices.

Such false authority opens the door to dissenting
voices,

creates fissures in hairline cracks.

Welcomes chaos into its home.

Writes its own defeat,

entering offensive and defensive phases when it must
not,

impeding forces with ignorance,

and burying its own corpse by misreading the enemy.

3.7 War demands worship before it will grant victory.

Recognise when to quietly walk away and when to sound the charge.

Know the mathematics of war and how this affects deployments.

Within all ranks of your forces ensure the same will is shared.

Exist in a constant state of preparedness,

anticipating your adversary even during unprecedented peace.

See even the trickle of poisoned words before the floodgates open.

Maintain the fulcrum against authority's hand-fetched disasters.

3.8 Worship of war grants triumph through wisdom old as time itself.

To know victory is to understand war,

to understand war is to know your enemy,

to know your enemy is to understand yourself,

to understand yourself is to know victory.

This is the strategy.

A comprehension of reflections.

The operating system.

It cannot be attacked.

Cannot be defeated.

A thousand battles will never be lost if you live by this code,

avoiding the black mirror of defeat.

Those who do not understand the strategy

will not know victory,

for they cannot understand war.

Those who do not understand war

cannot know their enemy

and will suffer defeat

when an adversary arrives unseen and unexpected,

despite the cacophony of the inevitable approach.

CONFIGURATION

4.1 Honoured,

in war,

is the insurance of one's own invincibility.

Protected,

fortified,

time is the only weapon an arsenal requires.

A careless adversary will become vulnerable

as grains trickle through the neck of the hourglass.

An indomitable existence solely yours to maintain,

in perpetuity.

Those skilled in war

choose to be impervious.

Create the unassailable.

Mould impregnability,

knowing they can never force an enemy to become
permeable.

Never attempt design of weakness.

Nor construct defencelessness.

Harvest that which exists.

The unskilled may understand victory's concept,

but will never taste its vintage,

for they do not know this disposition of war.

4.2 The wise drink deep,

for they master the formations.

Defence is invulnerable,

perfected by the projection of nothing.

Masked in layers,

solid as mountains.

Deep as ravines.

Attack is to lay oneself naked

and boast of everything.

Intangible as clouds,

incorporeal as smoke.

Night shadows.

The wise know the palate of these formations.

Understand the delicate flavours of triumph.

These wines flow most freely in victorious defence.

4.3 No true warrior bides inconsequential reports

of the acts of a dotard,

and shuns artless victory.

They pay no heed to low conflicts,

where satisfaction is attained with blood,

or ignorance,

or wildfire brawl.

There is no finesse and no praise for triumph attained
by these means.

No mark of wisdom for predicting the outcome in a
dullard's battle.

A firm grip measures no fortitude.

The plain view of an eclipse does not prove vision.

To hear peeling sirens is not evidence of listening.

The true warrior conquers with ease,

almost silently.

The whisper of time barely psithurism.

Their victory is plain,

and comes without omen:

is claimed without fortune

or ceremony.

Their triumph is perfect.

Irresistible.

The unbound conquest of enemies

defeated before lines were drawn.

The warrior stands in the mountains and the ravines,

flying from the shadows and the clouds,

surrendering no opportunity

presented by time.

4.4 The triumphant knows victory before war
commences.

The defeated pursues battle's bloodthirst alone,

success relegated to undefined afterthought.

Before conflict is awoken,

the skilled tend to the strategy.

Master wisdom of the formations.

Balance the scales.

The victorious measure their foe.

Measurement allows an estimation of the enemy.

Estimation permits a calculation of strength and
weakness.

Calculation informs a comparison against oneself.

Comparison defines victory or defeat.

These are the scales of war.

Triumph is the boulder weighed against the grain of sand.

The skilled harness victory and defeat this way,

before choosing the field upon which to win.

MEMORY

5.1 Remember:

the effective division of resource

is to conquer with many,

or few,

with equal ease.

Matters of the assembly of forces.

Measurement.

Estimation.

Calculation.

Comparison.

Deployment's foundations,

upon which the rallying dogwhistles and catcalls are designed.

5.2 Remember:

the three hands of war must always be accounted for.

Combining the acknowledged,

the detached,

and the deniable.

It is only by deploying these assets in balance,

a fighting force can claim perfect defensive victory,

without ever tasting defeat.

Balancing the scales,

harnessing this trinity,

an army will emerge triumphant in any conflict.

A sledgehammer on crystal.

Perfection is a direct assault by the force of all three,

but victory is only procured by their indirect
deployment.

Frictionless,

disembodied,

these hands softly strangle without raising arms.

5.3 Remember:

the art of war is to master the unattributable.

Circuitous engagements.

Sleight of hand,

building layers of distraction and blame unseen until
too late.

Hindrance of truth and reconciliation,

in futures not yet conceived.

Insidious lasting damage,

a lingering recollection of pain,

to deny with a smirk.

Leave only smoke to lash out at in reply.

5.4 Remember:

war is the exploitation of nature's imperfect creation.

For limited human perceptions birth a world

of sounds so numerous they remain unheard.

Colours so complex they exist unseen.

Flavours so varied they endure untasted.

Unknown human memory.

The artful warrior alone holds such knowledge,

and fights limitlessly.

Beyond the horizon,

saddling a tireless, forgotten beast.

War that can never be stopped.

Conflict beyond comprehension.

Warriors ride impossibility.

Infinity.

5.5 Remember:

tsunami carry cities.

The momentum of war is this.

Hummingbird moves his wings beyond the possibility of time.

Opportunity in war exists between those beats.

The warrior studies both.

Momentum the unstoppable force,

timing the immovable object.

The potential lies in their engineered collision.

Expansion.

An explosion of perfect energy,

in which lies control.

Power.

These reins of war,

when held,

generate calm amidst the battle,

and bring clear vision.

Blasts of ice to the heat of conflict,

permitting the conquest of the contrary.

5.6 In your own forces:

structure from chaos,

and bravery from terror.

Triumph in defeat.

In the adversary:

chaos from structure,

terror from bravery.

Defeat from triumph.

5.7 This is the memory of war.

Division.

Power.

Infinity.

Remember!

INSTALLATION

6.1 Be at war before war itself comes.

Lie in wait.

A sprung trap.

Coiled energy preserved.

Arrive at war late,

charging blind,

spent before battle is joined,

defeated.

6.2 The warrior is not raised,

in response to a conflict.

The warrior is conflict.

Lines and nets and lures never dry.

Both fisherman of enemies,

and the dam on his river.

The trawler reeling him in to perish,

and the collapsed bridge across retaliation's ravine.

Salmon traps and landslides in the mountain passes of
confrontation.

Both baiting an enemy,

and laying the boulders in their path.

Always.

6.3 Tire a rested foe,

run them from their sets and dens.

Chase them.

Hound them to exhaustion,

unrelenting.

Bring them to starvation,

when they are fat.

Disrupt supply and create panicked demand.

Deplete their reserves and own their replenishment.

Destabilise stability.

Shake the ground beneath their feet,

and create danger in safe spaces.

Turn their world on its head.

Herd them to their planned positions,

only to find you already waiting,

and simultaneously rally where they are undefended.

Duplicitous surprises at every turn.

Preserve your own strength by marching where no conflict yet lives,

conquering without battle,

grounds yet defined.

Pathfind.

But likewise defend yourself against such assault,

fortifying the unknown.

Fight on the fields of your own imagination to attain limitless victory.

Dream.

6.4 The true warrior attacks beyond the capability of defence,

and defends beyond the capability of attack.

The subtle,

deceitful,

silent,

mystery is the ruler of fate.

King of quiet advance beyond resistance,

assaulting and devouring voids.

Queen of lightning withdrawal beyond any chase,

6.6 See your enemy,

but remain unseen.

Display your enemy,

but remain unshown.

Dilute your enemy,

but remain unwatered.

Divide him as you multiply,

overwhelm his decimation with swollen numbers.

Spread your enemy thin,

through secrecy of your plans,

and creating myriad fronts with boasts.

Invent weapons and rumours of them,

fear where no risk exists,

to divert dwindling resources.

Prey on this weakness.

Strike viciously with the power of mass,

but with precision.

Attacking only few of the weakened lines,

in doing so trapping your foe into his eventual defeat.

Reinforcements draw the remaining fronts weaker

defended.

Attack again.

The cycle continues.

Attack again.

Defending everything is to defend nothing,

assuring your victory.

Triumph is built upon forcing your adversary to
prepare for you.

Defeat lies in the preparations of an obliged hand,

for they can never relent,

while unaware of where and when you will come,

and never regroup with any meaning when you do.

6.7 The warrior knows the enemy he stands against
better than himself.

Studies his best-laid plans and policies,

dissects his laws and his regulations.

Picks at the scabs in his society,

examines the infections and open wounds.

Understand his motivations,

both good and bad.

Document their driving forces,

and their inhibitions.

The innermost desires,

and the deepest buried fears,

are the grounds on which battles must be fought,

through each and every segment of an adversary's construction.

This is the key to both support and suppression.

Division and unity.

Manipulation through emotion more powerful than any truth.

Defence from this is easily engineered.

By existing without form,

without external scrutiny or understanding,

the same tactics cannot function against you.

Destroy the mechanisms by which you can be categorised.

Weed out the looking glasses through which your enemy can recognise you.

Be unfamiliar.

Alien.

Dangerous.

And render even espionage useless with fallacy.

Exist as deceit,

in constant flux.

Indescribable.

Unknowable.

6.8 Victory exists only as a changeling.

A fleeting shape in a passing cloud,

never to be replicated.

No set pieces bring continuous triumph.

Flow as the sea,

untenable pressure in your depths.

When they go high,

go lower still.

Crushing all.

Shaping yourself against the terrain of the enemy and bearing down,

rather than adapting to his peaks and troughs.

Over time,

reshape him,

grinding even his cliffs to sand.

Constant erosion.

An everlasting advance as formless as river water,

as poisonous to drink in as the ocean.

6.9 The art of war is to wax and wane as the moon,

harnessing the power of all tides.

COMMAND LINES

uncatchable.

Unarrestable.

6.5 To draw an enemy,

examine what he must rescue.

Study his obligations.

Outside of home's safe walls,

beyond easy range,

assault wherever he is duty bound to provide aid,

rendering domestic defences useless.

Create paper castles from stone,

by fighting far away.

To put down an enemy,

build an unassailable barrier from nothing.

A stand-off of terrifying power alone.

A threat of assured mutual destruction.

To provoke a grinding halt,

draw a line in smoke as solid as any fortification.

Project.

7.1 In hybrid warfare,

Acknowledged assets take orders from authority,

authority itself justified by the spiritual.

The acknowledged activate the detached and deniable,

casting dandelion seeds further and further still.

Weeds to inhibit healthy regrowth at eventual
discovery.

An asymmetric army is assembled this way,

silently gathered within the enemy's borders,

without camp-fire to raise alarm.

The favourable economics of silent running,

ensure the warrior's forces are gathered with seamless
ease,

no difficulty to arise until the hardwired command
lines are run.

Only then,

at execution,

will glitches appear,

and be written out.

7.2 The mastery of execution lies in making up down,

in left changed to right.

The democratic to crooked,

the state the deep swamp,

and the cheap criminal the Commander In Chief.

Perfection is found in:

making fortunes from created disadvantages,

shorting the society of the adversary,

and creating conspiracy fiction to obfuscate facts of conspiracy.

To allege collusion in order to collude.

To collude in order to make allegation.

Destroying sanction for capital gain,

by dispensing capital to remove sanction.

7.3 Be caught first,

but be captured quietly,

and only when and where it suits.

Taunt.

Be waiting ahead of the curve,

louder than ever,

gleeful,

and at your convenience.

This is to master execution.

7.4 Anticipate your failure,

accept its consequences,

before the command lines are run.

Bury your weaknesses and mitigate your damage,

by creating a world for yourself which exists beyond available punishment.

Live and thrive in the dark,

layering your defences,

through the detached and deniable.

And still ensure the acknowledged are little more than sacrifices,

ready to be made.

Final buck stops before your one unacceptable loss.

Be ruthless.

For in any war

gains may still see failures.

7.5 The prepared have escape mechanisms built in.

Kill switches.

Sandboxes.

The weapons of the true warrior.

Accept any advance will see collateral damage.

Financial,

tangible,

or human.

Account for these before any march of war.

Balance the tinderbox on the pillars.

Bleed money,

assets,

and people,

as a snake sheds its skin.

Understand that pace accelerates gain and loss in
unison.

Focus outlay on rapid advance,

accepting that investment in war is investment is death.

Only spend to die this way,

knowing mortality starts at home.

7.6 Extreme alliance is key to victory in execution,

so seek the extremes of political spectrum,

harness the bitter power of grievance.

Embrace the supremacists and the egotistical.

Find the monsters under the rocks.

Massage their dreams.

Feed their fears.

Arm them.

Know their hearts,

and buy them.

Compromise them in impossible holds.

Approach with friendly tongue,

or vile mouth as you must,

to harvest their fruit,

and propagate your lies.

The warrior is the malignant tumour,

corrupting the body it attacks.

An apex predator,

learning every step in the food-chain beneath it,

and sparing a few to gorge on an endless feast.

Tracking their hunts,

sharing their lairs,

acquiring intimate knowledge of the waterhole traffic,

which forms their ecosystem.

Devouring the weak around them through these
learnings,

before digesting them too.

Capitalise and exploit.

Exploit and capitalise.

The extreme are the servants of your assets,

unseen footsoldiers far removed.

Disposable,

beneath even the detached and deniable.

The first layer of sandpits and buck stops.

Your dandelion seeds.

7.7 Hybrid warfare is founded on this great deception,

of hospitality and shared vision,

of collusion,

and collision of ideals.

The creation of division through unity,

such unity possible because of existing division.

A catalyst in the engine of war -

a machine promising divided plunder,

annexation of lands,

implementation of managed democracies,

under oligarch control.

Set these lowly beasts upon your scales,

measure them,

and only ever ally with those found wanting.

7.8 Focus on your strategic communications,

for your assets must blindside the enemy without premature discovery.

Establish your signals:

the language of the forked tongue,

obscured in mud.

Encrypt with care,

decrypt with the appearance of recklessness.

Misinform without exception.

Disinform with precision.

Create sound and light when your messages are silent,

only the softest of whispers when plans are screamed.

Bury chalk marks in the digital world,

yet embed your designs on the street.

Hide the truth in the banal,

the critical behind the bland.

Be fancy.

Advertise the lies on the modern billboards,

attacking the weak overtly but without accountability.

Be cozy.

Savage outdated regulation,

and principles built upon adherence to rules,

by assaulting the national psyche with unstoppable chaos.

Be analytical.

Invoke emotion with the coldest of calm,

then disappear,

leaving only forensic fragments.

These are the command lines of war.

CODE

8.1 The truth of war,

of its art,

transcends the foundations of conflict upon which
nations deliberate.

The philosophies and statecrafts of confrontation are
not themselves warfare,

only elements of a whole.

The command lines a drop in conflict's ocean,

mastered by few.

Delivered with devastating effect by many less than
that.

To understand war is not to wage it.

To wage war is to understand everything.

This is the code by which war is fought and won.

8.2 Coalitions and free states,

treaties and partnerships,

unions,

present grave dangers.

Seas beyond your safe navigation,

built upon history and common goals.

Pomp and purpose.

Legal structures,

the wrecks to pierce your hull.

Reefs solid and thriving,

harbours of life,

and hubs in which all will gather.

Community.

Where these surround an enemy,

or themselves are your target,

their submission must be attained by the constant
battering of a storm force,

inflicting risk and threat and harm.

Intangible erosion and disturbance and tearing apart.

Cut off supply chains,

yet save them with provision too.

Murder in plain sight,

but with plausible deniability.

Out-voice their media and politics,

a friendly outsider with an alternative view.

Challenge the very fabric of established guard,

with little more than disarming smiles.

Survey their fragile structures,

and infest with malware.

Ravage cohesion with fear.

Erode.

Disturb.

Tear.

But only sufficiently to wholly occupy their attention,

without truly diminishing one's own capability.

A part-time investment -

a sideshow -

which does not engage their full or unified retaliation.

Petty diversions,

in truth,

leaving any primary objective attainable,

and your forces intact,

by avoiding pre-emption.

An unfathomable shadow of passing hull,

indistinct from below,

flags unseen.

Harnessing their inherent weaknesses with precision,

to profiteer elsewhere.

Then,

unchallenged,

preserve the junctions and couplings and passing
places,

havens and ports,

through your alignments with the extremists,

and installed oligarchs.

Reefs outlying reefs.

Sandbanks of your own making,

uncharted,

Creating control,

through manufactured bolt-holes,

and hand-carved safe passage.

8.3 The warrior understands there are no beaten paths,

for you must make your own.

Survey and poll,

chart.

Adapt the communities to suit your will,

and own the world in doing so.

This is hybrid warfare,

and in it no way is barred.

No reach too long to land a blow.

The pathfinder knows there are commands of authority
to be shunned.

Ignored.

Dismissed.

For the true warrior exists beyond authority,

though he understands its pillar.

Sails freely over conflict's rough surface and

away from accountability,

a ghost ship.

Do not set down on awkward ground.

Leave no marks in the sand.

Never rest where you hold the strings to no puppets.

Pass as lightning through such unsafe territories,

and idle only when entrenched,

when encircled,

to reacquaint with the strategy of war.

To reflect,

and write out glitches from the command lines.

To re-perfect and adapt your execution.

8.4 The mindful warrior,

with knowledge of war's code,

weighs profit against risk.

Balances serious harm against immediacy of every threat.

Maps the unmappable.

Draws his own terrain on dark alliance.

Damping his own desires -

cravings for spoils,

and infliction of harm -

to arrive at victory' goal,

and avoid disaster.

Only the reckless cowards,

those blinded by rage,

the guilty and shameful,

those beholden to their assets,

are lost.

Doomed to the crushing depths,

unseeing of risks,

unknowing of threats.

Unaware of immediacies,

their traits are cursed in war,

defeat assured again and again.

8.5 Be ever alert,

to the slow suffocating sieges avoided as plague,

territory and grounds upon which contest is always sure oblivion.

Of the wrecks and rocks,

and the ports and passages leading to triumph.

Only where inevitable,

where dry river beds await blood torrents,

will you enter into direct battle.

DEVICES

9.1 A globe unprepared for the internet,

an existence without filter,

education barely adequate,

for cohesion in the close quarters of urban sprawl,

has freed no one.

Equity and justice still absent,

the fortified walls of privilege lines as firm as ever.

The evolution of conflict through connectivity,

the greatest of war's allies,

creating a borderless terrain,

without reflection in law and treaty.

A culture of sleepless information,

volume collapsing the mechanisms nations relied upon
for defence of the mind.

Segmentation and microtargeting,

destroying the psyche itself.

This is the terrain of the warrior.

Disinformation a weapon,

sharpened to slice falling silk.

Traps and illusions,

wedges and maps.

the devices of war.

No sword or gun or rifle,

no pack to carry.

Light adaptability no drain to stamina,

the new kingdom is designed for warfare.

9.2 The connected world is your mountain,

the high camp from which all is seen.

All views open.

And all hostile actions downhill.

In the new terrain you are mountain warfare.

Your world is the river,

the unassailable mid stream,

the flow against which no advance can be made,

yet also the safe crossing and high banks.

You are river warfare.

Your world is the salt marsh,

the rapid,

unlingering assault close to vegetation,

trees to your back.

You are marshland warfare.

You are the level ground,

death always at your vanguard,

life safe behind.

Legends of emperors powdered to the dust of irrelevance,

in this new landscape.

The warrior unchained from convention.

9.3 There is no high ground,

so attack lower than they dare dream.

No necessity exists to nurture,

so in this new world destroy freely.

Discovery is no hindrance,

for the land will bend and yield as you command.

The swell of winter runoff in the mountains no longer halts your valley crossings,

seasons as irrelevant as tales of old.

With the waterfall at your command,

the sheer cliffs of the enemy,

are no challenge.

All can be written around your adversary where he stands,

And re-written and re-written and re-written.

So reshape at your will.

Terraform.

to form terror.

9.4 Explore every facet of this uncharted terrain,

not to seek signs of ambush,

or the dens of spies,

but to ambush and spy upon them.

Phish and hack and deny service.

Infiltrate grids and distribution centres,

laying sprung traps,

and creating backdoors.

Provide protection from viral infection,

while exfiltrating and infesting,

harvesting communications and information,

to compromise with later.

This is how you will redesign the landscape around
your enemy again and again.

Then,

when your enemy makes no move,

attack his strength with the weaknesses you have
discovered.

When he advances,

block his way with boulders of his compromise,

and lead him down the blind alleys to defeat.

9.5 In the borderless world,

they cannot lure you,

because you are already there.

They cannot perplex and confuse,

because you are the reeds behind which they hide.

When your firewall alarms burst to song,

wingbeats of warning from the silence,

it is too late because your networks are dead.

Petrified remnants.

No ambush is possible,

because you have moved the grounds under their very

feet.

9.6 Bleed them of knowledge,

as they suckle on endless data.

Reap this harvest to read their signs.

The spending in excess,

the mark of a desperate foe.

Austerity and punishment,

the sign of a weary nation's death.

Ignorance of war through both tyranny,

and conciliatory tone,

omens of your victory and their defeat.

9.7 In the sleepless world of information,

always be humble in your words,

so they know you are attacking them.

Always be strong with your words,

as you leave the field victorious.

Tell them you are coming,

with ceremony and display.

Let them see your decoys,

by advancing and retreating everywhere they look.

And show them easy wins,

to confirm your knowledge of their incapacity,

when they fail to engage.

Give them promise of treaty and cooperation,

to signal the strike of a final blow.

9.8 Set your traps,

cast your illusions,

drive your wedges,

and redraw your maps.

Create an indecipherable world of nonsense,

from which nothing can be gleaned,

for these are the devices with which the prizes of war
are won.

But mind the warriors who simply bide time,

unmoved by your efforts,

neither retreating nor advancing.

For they share your kingdom.

NETWORKS

10.1 The connected world is built upon a series of networks,

the channels through which the devices of war are deployed.

The accessible,

the public,

the insecure,

the protected,

the encrypted,

the masked,

and the dark.

10.2 An accessible network faces front,

tools to enter at the fingertips of all,

in our hands and pockets and bags.

On our desktops.

From browser,

to game system,

to telephone,

to tablet,

every hour of every day.

Open.

The accessible network is the key to war,

and the pieces of ourselves we place there,

the warrior's greatest hybrid weapon.

All conflict begins here.

10.3 The public network is the repository of all humanity.

Social,

business,

pleasure.

Beckoning us with community,

becoming our daily lives,

usurping the reality outside of the window.

Usage encouraged,

pages sponsored,

advertising dark and light,

tantalising us with clickbait.

Exploiting our pliability.

Surveying constantly to harvest our souls.

Through this network we know the world,

and the world knows us.

This is where warriors learn our weaknesses,

as we become bytes and bits,

re-assembled as data points.

Thousands of glistening give-aways,

our small treasures combined,

made whole,

until we are understood better than we even
comprehend ourselves.

Public networks are the source of big data,

by which we hand over all power.

The insidious force behind our voluntary surrender,

before conflict is even recognised.

10.4 The insecure network awaits a parasite to host.

Invites intrusion,

exfiltration,

insertion,

and hijack.

Lays open the routes by which processing power is borrowed,

by which infections are spread,

allowing the creation of masks.

And insecurity is fluid,

evolving.

From router,

to virtual machine,

to the inane:

the internet of things creating monsters from white goods.

The power of denial,

disruption,

and destruction

in the homes of millions.

Unchecked.

Discoverable within minutes.

Open windows through which war silently creeps.

10.5 The protected network exists to be probed,

tested,

phished,

and broken.

Weak passwords,

guessable by machine.

Pliable humans surrendering the keys,

to familiar communications.

Attachments.

Messages.

The contact we crave.

These networks are as weak as the users they host,

protection itself a sign of worthy target -

possession of information of value.

Power here is through knowledge of what is held,

and theft of that which can be leaked to tactical
advantage.

10.6 The encrypted network is the bane of authority,

frustrating intrusion,

legitimate and illegitimate.

A tool to many,

by which safety and privacy are secured,

yet a weapon to many more,

by which blood is shed and plans made.

One the scale a force for good

weighed in balance against terror,

the encrypted network must be broken,

by all nations.

For war is fought and won by enigma.

The ability to know secrets.

Encrypted networks are life and death to warfare,

and their very existence a conflict too.

A flashpoint of division to exploit.

10.7 The masked network is the tool of the warrior,

the ability to come and go unseen.

Easy to establish,

impossible to see beyond,

a traceless escape into which fallacy can be interwoven.

No address to identify,

no location to pinpoint,

the mask never slips.

And this network can shift reality,

placing bombs where no target exists,

or ships where another occupies a lane.

Creating misses or hits at will,

traffic where no traffic exists.

The masked network is art.

Unattributable ghost soldiers,

discovered by sweat alone.

Or sheer luck.

A weapon of extreme precision,

made of lethal pretence.

10.8 The dark network sits below all,

an underworld,

existing on borrowed infrastructure.

The marketplace for data's harvest,

the home of peddlers and hackers,

and a criminal state beneath our feet.

Borderless,

unbound,

fat through cryptocurrency,

impregnable by its nature.

Inaccessible.

Secure.

Encrypted.

Masked.

This network is the warrior's playground.

10.9 The seven networks are elemental in hybrid
warfare.

Launchpad,

testing ground,

arms dealership,

and delivery mechanism.

Through them conflict flows freely,

unstoppable.

The warrior's duty is to exist within them,

shape them.

Harness each of them.

For strength in numbers means nothing,

capability of leadership is rendered useless,

and no army can decay in wait.

Through these networks,

the warrior knows his enemy better than he knows
himself,

conquers with emotion,

uses the adversary's tools and weapons against him,

hides in plain sight,

and leaves without a trace.

The seven networks are war's perfection,

arising from a species' need for togetherness.

A weakness from a crowning strength.

Collusion against the common good,

dressed as collaboration.

The best of intentions,

the most powerful weapon in history.

10.10 To the future,

the legacy of hybrid war.

Machine learning.

Conflict out of the hands of humanity,

infesting the seven networks and growing more
powerful with time alone.

Automated efficiency,

artificial intelligence,

learning the art of hybrid war,

able to act faster than mankind ever could.

Already in the wild.

NODES

11.1 Through the networks war's devices reach the nodes,

the ends of the tendrils extending into the connected world.

The intersections through which detached and deniable assets meet the end users.

The recipients of the message.

The networks bring together the pillars of war,

and all of its philosophy,

while the junctions set war into action.

Both trophy and mechanism interwoven.

11.2 The warrior controls the nodes,

the bot,

the troll,

the hacker,

the spy,

the crisis actor,

the deceiver,

the useful fool,

and the innocent.

And,

in doing so,

controls victory.

11.3 The bot is the machine,

the child of technological advance,

now crawling,

but to run in the years which follow.

Simple lines of code,

automating responses,

creating volume and depth across the networks,

by spreading the message beyond the reach of partisan authority alone.

Once the scourge of the public network,

the bot has spread to infest almost all pathways,

invented characters wildly seeking connection and response.

It pushes the narrative,

to make nations great again,

saddles the dark secrets of network centrality,

to infect humanity with false desire.

Seeks the insecure,

to replicate.

To deny service,

and to stifle free thought,

creating illusions of consensus,

and falsifying the will.

A dispensable military,

tens of thousands of soldiers to lose without loss.

An army for hire and duplication,

created in minutes,

and replaced at will.

Pestilence on connectivity.

11.4 The troll is the ghost in the machine,

a disembodied human soul in spectral form.

A trick of the mind,

and grinning falsehood with human hands behind it.

Farmed,

managed,

collated,

curated,

the troll is a careful study of the enemy.

Executed perfectly,

in vast numbers,

waving familiar flags,

an army of liars,

presenting itself across the public networks,

wearing skin we recognise,

in order to destroy from within.

To spread dissent,

to whisper division,

and to learn and learn and learn.

An endless harvest of information,

reported back,

escalated,

digested,

developed,

and redeployed.

In duplicity,

black lives matter,

but blue lives matter,

but all lives matter.

Immigration will destroy you,

so immigrants must be bombed.

And what about this,

and what about that,

eroding down so it is up,

left so it becomes right,

and no faith in the person before you remains.

Until suspicion sits on every face,

and lies to every heart,

in every minute of its day.

11.5 The hacker is both fancy and cozy,

a reality and a lie when bare,

That with which you are familiar,

and that which is unrecognisable.

A white hat,

a grey hat,

a black hat.

Benign and malignant,

dressed anonymously behind a mask,

yet driven into spotlights to confuse.

The hacker you accept is the one in the news,

awaiting deportation,

extradition.

A boy in a bedroom.

The hacker you do not see exists behind versions of itself.

Plays with language and accent.

Is caught in advance,

but uncovered too late.

Discard the boy in the bedroom,

for the hacker of war has been and gone while you watch.

Your details phished,

your network penetrated,

information exfiltrated and sold in the dark.

Leaked by useful fools.

The hacker of war,

denies service to the media,

masks itself as dragons to ransom your health,

crashes your power networks,

and hijacks your processing power to create dark money.

The hacker of war hides within your protection,

extracting data,

secrets,

unseen until all is lost,

and the deceivers have riddled the world around you with conspiracy.

Beyond technical prowess,

beyond capture,

beyond failure,

the hacker is the God in the machine.

11.6 The spy is not what you believe it to be.

Neither troll nor deceiver,

the spy sits quietly,

unnoticed.

Hackers are but devices of spies,

who themselves garner not even a sideways glance,

and disappearing silently.

Waiting,

often idle,

within your institutions,

behind façades of respectability,

or even over your garden fence,

you have interacted with the spy.

You have freely given something away,

whether over network or in person,

or having shared the finest distillation with them,

forgetting their unmemorable face.

The spy is neither essential nor disposable,

nor to be trusted.

And they will never be recalled when the questions are quietly asked,

after the dust settles.

A unique breed,

the true warrior gives no credence to stated intent of a spy.

11.7 The crisis actor is an apparition.

A temporary phenomena,

deployed only in response to darkness,

to create disturbance.

Interchangeable,

the crisis actor can take any form.

Troll, bot, or human.

As an injured person,

one suffering grief,

or one who reports relatives missing during an incident.

They plant falsehood around victims,

create disruption in truth,

display false emotion.

Dark performance art,

and little more,

designed to exhaust and manufacture disarray,

by creating alternative truths,

before quieting once more,

and moving on to the next and the next and the next.

The crisis actor is the ultimate tool in an information war, which preys on fear and prejudice.

11.8 The deceiver exists not by accident,

but careful design.

A scheme of delicate development,

an organisation of media,

or respected voice within it.

A brand which outwardly prides itself on difference,

or unbiased truth no one else will tell,

its core a lava of planned deception.

Seeded carefully,

funded by nations,

separated by independent production,

the deceiver buys dissenting voices,

from familiar mouths.

Provides platform to the low standing,

to enhance views which suit the ends of the warrior.

A machine of foreign policy,

founded within the mechanics of conflict,

the deceiver is at war in the homes of the enemy,

each and every day.

The deceiver comes as a friend,

slowly poisoning minds,

while growing in popularity and acceptance.

A tumour of purposeful lies.

11.9 The useful fool is essential in hybrid war,

for without them the message cannot be turned
inwards,

against an adversary.

The fool is the familiar mouth,

the weapon of the deceiver,

the victim of the spy,

the tool of the hacker,

bolstered by bots,

and supported by trolls.

The dissenting voice,

the local character.

Plucky businessman,

political figure,

freedom fighter.

The compromised buffoon.

Where there is agenda,

or where a person is hard done by,

or where an ego is dented,

or a law is broken,

the useful fool can be found.

Selected for flaws,

greed,

and appetite,

the useful fool can be turned at the drop of a hat,

by soothing voice or threat,

to do the bidding of the warrior.

Deployed with strategic care,

they can bring about a nation's downfall,

by act of tremendous self-harm -

eroding the authority of an enemy with even a simple question.

It is more effective to force the enemy to eat itself,

at the instruction of the village idiot,

than to fight one thousand battles against common sense.

The useful fool is the greatest device of all.

11.10 The innocents are the people,

the most devastating of all weapons.

Swayed by bots,

by the urge to herd and belong.

Divided,

made suspicious of one another by trolls.

Attacked by hackers.

Duped by spies.

Triggered by crisis actors,

and driven to emotional response.

Softly persuaded,

accepting the alternative facts of the deceiver.

And complicit with the useful fool,

cannibalising themselves in reply.

The destruction of defences,

the surrender.

All networks lead to the people,

the innocents,

and the desired output of all nodes is their complicity
in self-destruction.

11.11 These are the routes to a subtle victory of
compliance,

without great cost.

The vectors for delivery of hybrid war's virus.

A code attacking the human mind.

Malware for the soul.

And it spreads across the networks by the eight nodes,

until all is consumed and victory is attained,

on and offline.

DENIAL OF SERVICE

12.1 As fire was the tool of pre-history,

denial is the burning of a city in the modern day.

12.2 There are five ways to deny service,

to maim an adversary in hybrid conflict.

These targeting concepts are as old flames:

people,

supplies,

equipment,

reserves,

communications.

Such an attack requires only limited resource,

will devastate within hours,

and can begin on a whim.

12.3 To warn an enemy,

deny service to its democracy.

Show strength by closing down registrations at critical times,

or by rendering its counting machines useless.

Create news,

but show only a masked hand outwardly,

while bragging to authority with a hushed smirk.

Making them fearful and complicit,

and the public discovery of final truth irrelevant,

by forced collusion.

12.4 To threaten an enemy,

deny service to health and transport and finance
temporarily.

Fill their headlines and networks with worry,

the urge to cry.

Stories of potential threats to life and limb.

But bury your action in foreign tongues,

misunderstood by most,

and laced with false attribution.

Even claim victimhood,

lying openly with a clear smile on your face,

rendering authority's acceptance an eventual deceit,

which will never be repeated to the people -

an act of unforgivable collaboration itself.

12.5 To disrupt an enemy,

deny service to its news networks,

disorientating the people with sudden and unfilled
silence,

to generate panic.

As the rising tide tightens its grip,

and they turn to public networks,

the social crutches,

deny service there too.

Force them to spoken word,

overloading outdated lines and exchanges with sudden
peak in demand,

creating engaged tones without lifting a hand,

and bringing sufferance upon the economy without
attacking it.

12.6 To scare an enemy,

deny service to its power network.

Shut down physical pipelines,

knowing how much they hold in reserve,

and running them down to critical levels.

Attack the automated junctions and refineries and distribution centres,

remotely switching off systems through control of controls.

Limit supply to trickle feed,

or overload ageing grids with surge,

causing failures otherwise beyond your reach.

Occupy repair crews,

and continue,

reducing capability without directly assaulting resource.

Leaving the lights off,

homes cold,

and food rotting where it is stored.

12.7 To attack an enemy,

deny service to its military,

by disabling its knowledge of location.

Render a navy and airforce useless by disrupting targeting and navigation.

Misplace troops and machines through GPS
manipulation.

And engage forces on far away fronts,

by creating false wars,

and required moral interventions.

Spread them thin,

draw and lure.

Above all,

silently develop new capability,

beyond their expertise,

leaving generals to ask for bullets and bombs,

while you fight with code and disinformation.

12.8 To destroy an enemy,

deny service in layers.

Disrupt on top of threat,

scare on top of that.

Attack still.

Sustain the denial.

And,

as the panic spills out of front doors,

and there is nowhere to turn,

isolate them completely and bring them to their knees.

Cut the undersea cables which connect them to the world.

Explode the pipelines which bring oil and gas.

Render them silent,

empty.

Defeated without troop deployment.

Economy destroyed for decades in hours.

Crushed.

A husk nation able to survive no longer than five days,

forcing it to be saved,

either by grovelling before allies,

or by conceding to your annexation and accepting servitude in perpetuity.

12.9 Critical infrastructure in the connected world is fragile,

unaffected by seasons or weather as fire once was.

No moon or Gods to appease,

all variables are reduced by necessity of economy,

communication,

and constant demand.

The greatest achievements of the human civilisation,

reflected in its fatal weakness.

MALWARE

13.1 Malware is the infestation of the adversary's psyche.

The constant harvest of data,

and its re-assembly for use with the devices of war,

quietly and insidiously infecting the networks,

and attacking the nodes,

without resort to outright denial of service.

The key to war,

the virus at the fingertips of the warrior,

and the grandest of all prizes in conflict.

But it cannot be used without restraint.

Must not be used without contemplation.

Mutating if handled improperly,

it is as likely to destroy a warrior as his enemy,

without respect for its power.

Investment in malware is the purchase of spies,

and fools,

and networks,

and nodes,

to silently deceive and persuade the enemy to consume itself.

Expenditure here is a display of a warrior's ultimate wisdom,

facilitating victory with ease,

and calculated precision.

Intimate a knowledge of a nation,

cannot come without prudent study of these elements.

Division cannot come from divination,

targeting of weakness does not arise from guesswork,

chaos cannot be brought about by luck.

13.2 Malware is the heart of hybrid war,

a viral attack on the soul of enemy,

destroying the pillars:

the message,

the spiritual,

the authority,

the reality,

and the discipline.

Rendering states inert,

and enfeebled.

13.3 War fought this way,

whether on foundations of dark money or open economy,

does not erode the public purse,

and creates the endless marches of multiple campaigns,

without the burdens known by the past.

Protracted conflict rendered to history,

without massed troops to accommodate,

or hide under tarpaulin,

No strains on the homefront,

to embitter the people,

and erode their curated will.

13.4 In days gone by,

spies were integral to the secret machinations of the hostile state,

but such singular notions are dead languages.

The dispositions of the adversary are now gleaned,

and manipulated,

by the totality of malware.

Tradition eclipsed by its dark whole.

There is no local knowledge which cannot be accessed,

for the world has been woven small.

There is no internal knowledge which cannot be hacked or phished,

for the networks are always as pliable as the human users.

There is no value in double agents,

untrusted relics,

unwanted in hybrid warfare,

usurped by advances.

There are no dead spies,

because disinformation is passed openly,

a merciless weapon in of itself,

trained everywhere with devastating capability.

There are no live spies,

because information travels faster than man,

and shifts on its journey.

rendering traditional espionage a mule racing against thoroughbreds.

Irrelevant secrets consigned to history.

13.5 In contemporary conflict,

justice,

humanity,

injustice,

and dehumanisation,

are balanced forces.

Relevant and irrelevant at once.

The concepts of each requiring full understanding,

yet demanding equal disregard.

Ruthless delivery,

of respectful maleficence and abusive benignity,

the malware harnessed by the warrior.

This is fighting at the crest of the waterfall.

Denial of defence and attack beyond limitation.

Infinity.

The doctrine of hybrid war.

DRIP WITH HONEY.

DIVIDE WITH WHISPERS.

DISRUPT WITH MADNESS.

CONQUER WITH VELVET.

Cynefin
R⬛AD

Lightning Source UK Ltd.
Milton Keynes UK
UKHW01f1000140618
324158UK00009B/86/P